The Nativity
Activity & Coloring Book

Yuko Green

Dover Publications
Garden City, New York

NOTE

An exciting way for kids to read the Christmas story, this book is packed with word searches, mazes, spot-the-differences, and other activities featuring Mary, Joseph, the Baby Jesus, and other key figures from the nativity. Complete with bible verses written in easy-to-understand language for kids, this book is an engaging way to celebrate the Christmas season. Solutions for the activity pages begin on page 39.

Copyright
Copyright © 2013 by Yuko Green
All rights reserved.

Bibliographical Note
The Nativity Activity and Coloring Book is a new work, first published by Dover Publications in 2013.

International Standard Book Number
ISBN-13: 978-0-486-49717-4
ISBN-10: 0-486-49717-8

Manufactured in the United States of America
49717812
www.doverpublications.com

A GIRL WHO LOVED GOD

A long time ago, **God** sent an **angel** to a young girl named **Mary**.
"God chose you to be the **mother** of a very special **baby**; God's
Son," said the angel, "his name will be **Jesus**." (Luke 1:26 - 35)

WITH GOD

with God.

Use the shape code to find out what the angel said to Mary about God. Write the letters in the blanks to spell it out.

(Luke 1:37)

ANOTHER MESSAGE

Write the opposite of each word on the blanks. Then write the circled letters, in order, to complete the puzzle below.

sorrow ◯ __ __ __

in ◯ __ __ __

fast ◯ __ __ __ __

right __ ◯ __ __ __

down __ ◯ __

day __ __ __ __ ◯ __ __

An angel appeared to ◯ ◯ ◯ ◯ ◯ ◯ __ __ __ __ __ __ ,

to whom Mary was engaged to be married. The angel said Mary was going to have a baby, God's Son. (Matthew 1:20)

3

THE TRIP TO FAR AWAY

Write the first letter of each picture in the box next to it. Then read the word to find out the name of Joseph's hometown.

Right before the baby was born, Joseph and Mary had to go on a long trip from their tiny country village of Nazareth to Joseph's hometown. (Luke 2:4)

A LONG JOURNEY

Help Mary and Joseph find the way to Bethlehem.

Nazareth

start

end

Bethlehem

Joseph and Mary went on a long journey from the town of Nazareth to the town of Bethlehem.

(Luke 2:1-5)

NO PLACE TO STAY

Fill in the puzzle with names of animals in the stable.

Bethlehem was crowded with many people. There was no room for Mary and Joseph at the inn.

The innkeeper said, "You can stay in a stable where I keep my animals." (Luke 2:6-7)

FIRST CHRISTMAS

That night, Mary's special baby was born. Mary wrapped her newborn baby in cloths and laid Him in a manger—a feeding box. (Luke 2:6-7) This was the first Christmas.

JOYFUL SONGS

Baa-baa, Hee-hew, Moo-o-o-o; joyful songs for a special baby.
These stable animals in each row look alike, but they are not.
Find and circle the sheep, donkey, and cow that is not the same
as the others in each group.

9

AN ANGEL

In the nearby hills, while shepherds were watching their sheep, an angel came to them and said, "I bring you good news of great joy that will be for everyone." (Luke 2:10)

GOOD NEWS

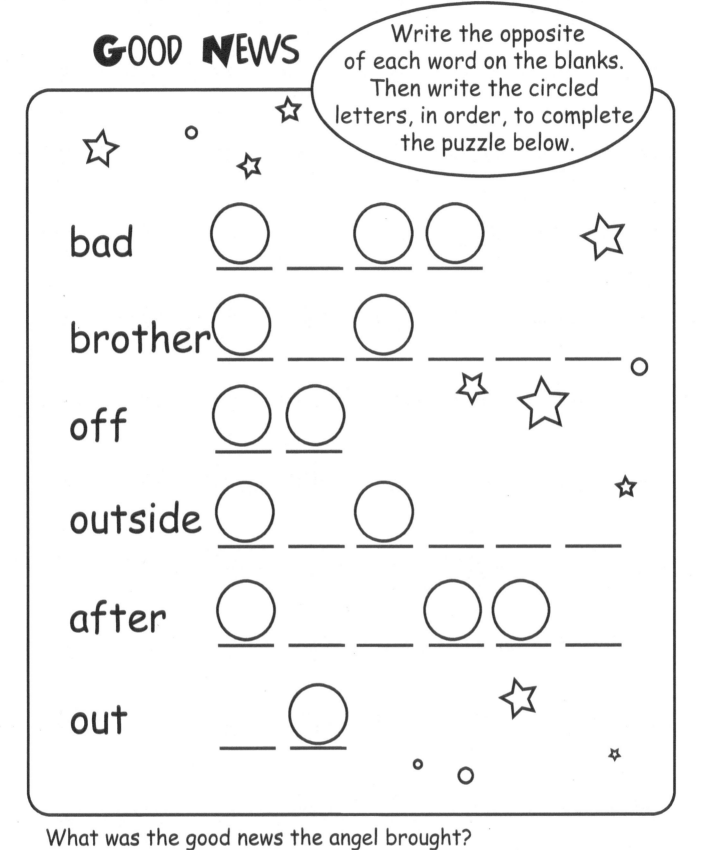

Write the opposite of each word on the blanks. Then write the circled letters, in order, to complete the puzzle below.

bad

brother

off

outside

after

out

What was the good news the angel brought?

in Bethlehem tonight. (Luke 2:10-12)

11

GREAT JOY

Angels appeared all around, praising God and singing, "Glory to God, and peace to all on earth."
(Luke 2:13-14)

After the angels were gone, the shepherds hurried to Bethlehem. There in the stable, they found the baby wrapped in a cloth, lying in a manger, just as the angel told them. "Our Savior is born," they said. (Luke 2:15-20)

13

THE SHEPHERDS FIND JESUS

The shepherds were the first ones to hear this good news!
They arrived to find the baby just as the angel had said.
Their hearts began to sing! (Luke 2:16)

This picture looks the same as the one on the opposite page, but it's not! Find and circle 10 things that are different.

BABY JESUS

How many words can you make using the letters in **Baby Jesus**?

bus _____

_____   _____

_____   _____

_____   _____

_____   _____

After the shepherds found the baby, they told everyone what the angel had said to them about this child. Seven days later, the baby was named Jesus. (Luke 2:15-21)

Jesus Is Born

◇ =a   ■ =c   ● =d   ☆ =e   ☽ =g

♡ =h   ❤ =l   △ =n   ○ =o   ▯ =t   ◆ =v

He came from

___ ___ ___ ___ ___ ___ to
♡   ☆   ◇   ◆   ☆   △

___ ___ ___ ___ ___ us
▯   ☆   ◇   ■   ♡

about ___ ___ ___ and
     ☽   ○   ●

His ___ ___ ___ ___ .
   ❤   ○   ◆   ☆

Jesus was a special baby, God's Son. He is also called the Savior, the Lord, King, Christ, and Messiah. Use the shape code and write the letters on the blanks to find out why Jesus was born.

A SPECIAL STAR

Find the special star by crossing out every star that appears more than once.

God made a special star appear in the sky far away in the East, as a sign to other people to let them know of the birth of the Savior. The Magi, the great wise men, saw the special star.

(Matthew 2:1-2)

THE NEWBORN KING

To find out the name of the town the Magi visited, fill in the missing letter of each picture. Then, read the word you have made from top to bottom.

ar

h   art

t   ee

s   n

tar

ngel

amp

sh   ep

oon

So Magi from the East came to _____, and asked, "Where is the one who was born king of the Jews? We saw his star and have come to worship him." (Matthew 2:1-2)

19

THROUGH THE DESERT

I am an animal who lives in deserts. The fat in my hump allows me to survive a long time without food. I am a big help to people traveling through the desert. Connect the dots from 1 to 45 to see my picture.

FOLLOW THAT STAR!

Help the Magi follow the special star to find Jesus in Bethlehem.

Jerusalem

start

end

Bethlehem

The Magi followed the star of God to Bethlehem. The star stopped over the house where they saw the child (Jesus) with his mother Mary. (Matthew 2:9-12)

THE VISIT OF THE MAGI

When the Magi saw the Christ child with his mother Mary, their hearts filled with joy. The Magi got down on their knees and worshiped the child of God. (Matthew 2:11)

This picture looks the same as the one on the opposite page, but it's not! Find and circle 10 things that are different.

GIFTS FOR THE KING

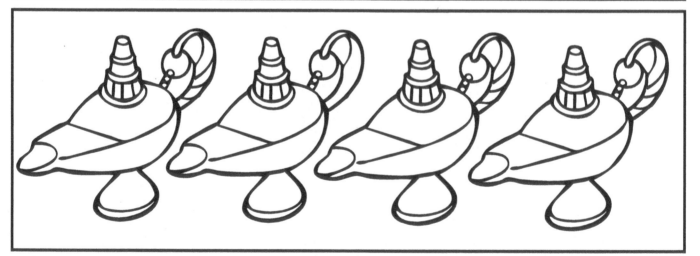

The magi gave Jesus special gifts of frankincense, gold, and myrrh. (Matthew 2:10-12) Find and circle the one gift in each row that looks different from the others.

KING HEROD

Help the Magi find a way home so they won't see King Herod.

Home

King Herod was angry. He wanted to be the only king. The Magi were given a warning in a dream, "Do not go back to King Herod." The king wanted to find baby Jesus and have him killed.

(Matthew 2:12)

25

LITTLE TOWN OF BETHLEHEM

Fill in the missing letters for each word. Then use those letters to complete the puzzle below.

__hr__stmas
①   ②

Birth__a__
③   ④

N__ti__ity
⑤   ⑥

s__ar
⑦

Bethlehem, the birthplace of Jesus, is called the

___ ___ ___ ___ of ___ ___ ___ ___ ___
① ② ⑦ ④   ③ ⑤ ⑥ ② ③

26

Unscramble each word and draw a line to its matching picture.

BAYB

_____

MYAR

_____

MNAEGR

_____

SATR

_____

AGNEL

_____

LMAB

_____

NATIVITY CROSSWORD

Use the picture clues on the next page to complete the crossword puzzle.

Across

3. Son of God
5. Heavenly messenger from God
6. They take care of sheep
8. Mary's husband
9. Where the infant Jesus slept
10. Wise men

Down

1. Mother of Jesus
2. The town where Jesus was born
4. This appeared in the sky over Bethlehem and guided the Magi to Jesus
7. Building that houses animals; where Jesus was born

star

angel

Bethlehem

stable

Mary

Jesus

Joseph

manger

shepherds

Magi

DONKEY

Find and circle the two donkeys that are exactly same.

Riding on a donkey was the most common way to travel during Bible times.

CHRISTMAS

How many words can you make using the letters in **Christmas?**

cat
_____

_____   _____

_____   _____

_____   _____

_____   _____

                    _____

                    _____

                    _____

As God showed his love to us by sending his son, Jesus, Christmas is the time for us to give and show our love to others.

CHRISTMAS
word search

Find and circle all 16 words below in the puzzle. The words go across, backward and down.

```
              A
          D   J   T
      S   T   A   R   S
    H   I   J   G   E   B   I
  C   A   N   E   S   E   A   C   F
          G   S   K   L   B
      N   M   U   G   N   I   K
    J   O   Y   S   O   R   R   P   O
  S   E   C   H   R   I   S   T   M   A   S
      A   N   G   E   L   H   T
    G   I   F   T   S   D   D   V   C
  L   Y   T   I   V   I   T   A   N   A   B
G   O   D   F   A   M   I   L   Y   B   A   B   C
          E   D   O
          F   H   V
          I   G   E
```

ANGEL	CHRISTMAS	JESUS	NATIVITY
CANES	FAMILY	JOY	SING
BABY	GIFTS	KING	STAR
BIRTHDAY	GOD	LOVE	TREE

32

NATIVITY JIGSAW PUZZLE

Color, cut, and make your own Nativity jigsaw puzzle.

CHRISTMAS CARD

Color, cut, and fold to make your own Christams card.

Wishing you
a Merry Christmas!

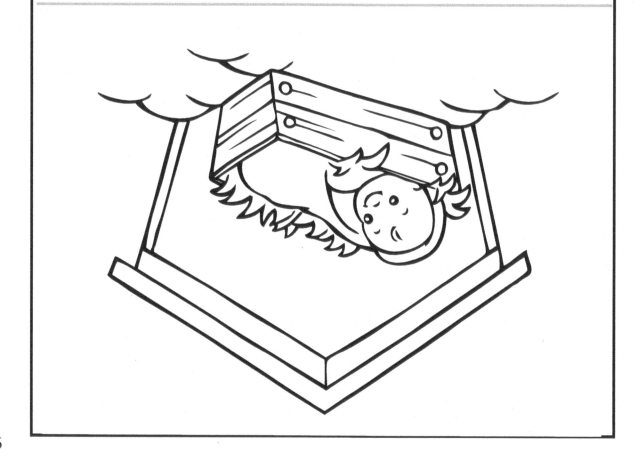

NATIVITY MAP

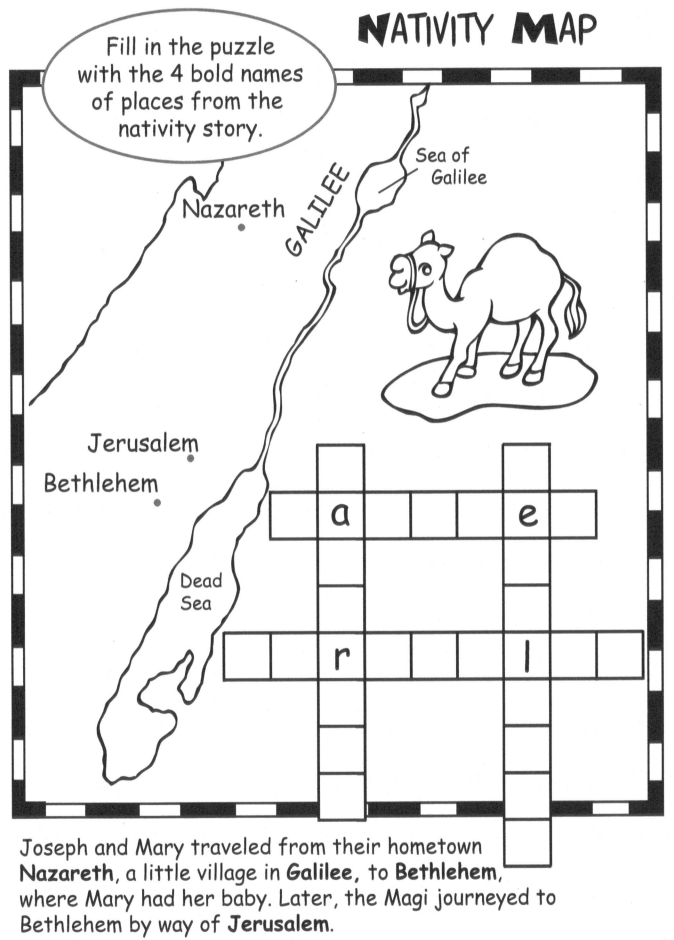

Fill in the puzzle with the 4 bold names of places from the nativity story.

Sea of Galilee

GALILEE

Nazareth

Jerusalem

Bethlehem

Dead Sea

a   e

r   l

Joseph and Mary traveled from their hometown **Nazareth**, a little village in **Galilee**, to **Bethlehem**, where Mary had her baby. Later, the Magi journeyed to Bethlehem by way of **Jerusalem**.

SOLUTIONS

A Girl Who Loved God

Find and circle the 7 bold words from the story in the puzzle box. Look across, down, and diagonally.

```
X M Y G B X P
A M A Z A F A
L O R B B I N
G O T X G G E
E U N X H G E
C B E O Y E S
K J E S U S S
```

Let everything happen just as you said.

With God

☆=b ■=e ●=g
☽=h □=i ♡=l
♥=m ◇=n ▲=o
○=p ▯=s △=t

N o t h i n g   i s
◇ ▲ △ ☽ □ ◇ ● □ ▯

i m p o s s i b l e
□ ♥ ○ ▲ ▯ ▯ □ ☆ ♡ ■

with God.

page 1

page 2

Another Message

Write the opposite of each word on the blanks. Then write the circled letters, in order, to complete the puzzle below.

sorrow (j) o y
in (o) u t
fast (s) l o w
right l (e) f t
down u (p)
day n i g (h) t

An angel appeared to (J) (o) (s) (e) (p) (h)

page 3

The Trip to Far Away

Write the first letter of each picture in the box next to it. Then read the word to find out the name of Joseph's home town.

B
e
t
h
l
e
h
e
m

page 4

39

A LONG JOURNEY

Help Mary and Joseph find the way to Bethlehem.

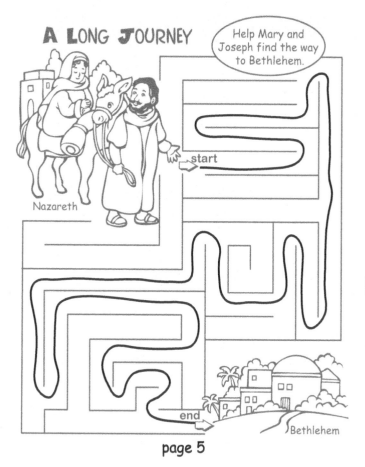

start

Nazareth

end

Bethlehem

page 5

NO PLACE TO STAY

Fill in the puzzle with names of animals in the stable.

pages 6-7

FIRST CHRISTMAS

Find and circle all the letters in **CHRISTMAS** hidden in the picture below.

page 8

JOYFUL SONGS

page 9

GOOD NEWS

Write the opposite of each word on the blanks. Then write the circled letters, in order, to complete the puzzle below.

bad — (g) o (o) d

brother — (s) i (s) t e r

off — (o) (n)

outside — (i) n (s) i d e

after — (b) e f (o) r e

out — i (n)

What was the good news the angel brought?

(G) (o) (d) (s) (s) (o) (n) (i) (s) (b) (o) (r) (n)

page 11

GREAT JOY

Find and circle the two angels that look exactly the same.

page 12

Help the shepherds find their way to Bethlehem.

LET'S GO TO BETHLEHEM!

start

end

page 13

pages 14-15

41

BABY JESUS

How many words can you make using the letters in Baby Jesus?

bus

yes   say

busy   sea

easy   buy

us   be

               base ...

page 16

JESUS IS BORN

◇ =a   ■ =c   ● =d   ☆ =e   ☽ =g

♡ =h   ♥ =l   △ =n   ○ =o   ▯ =t   ◆ =v

He came from

h e a v e n to
♡ ☆ ◇ ◆ ☆ △

t e a c h us
▯ ☆ ◇ ■ ♡

about G o d and
       ☽ ○ ●

His l o v e .
     ♥ ○ ◆ ☆

page 17

A SPECIAL STAR

Find the special star by crossing out every star that appears more than once.

page 18

THE NEWBORN KING

To find out the name of the town the magi visited, fill in the missing letter of each picture. Then read the word you have made from top to bottom.

	J	ar
h	**e**	art
t	**r**	ee
s	**u**	n
	s	tar
	a	ngel
	l	amp
sh	**e**	ep
	m	oon

page 19

42

Through the Desert

page 20

Follow That Star!

Help the Magi follow the special star to find Jesus in Bethlehem.

Jerusalem

start

end

Bethlehem

page 21

pages 22-23

Gifts for the King

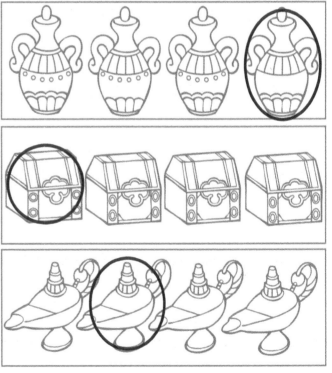

page 24

KING HEROD

Help the Magi find a way home so they won't see King Herod.

Home

page 25

LITTLE TOWN OF BETHLEHEM

Fill in the missing letters for each word. Then use those letters to complete the puzzle below.

C̲hri̲s̲tmas
①   ②

Birth d̲a̲y̲
③ ④

N̲a̲ti̲v̲ity
⑤   ⑥

s̲t̲ar
⑦

Bethlehem - the birthplace of Jesus, is called the

C̲i̲t̲y̲ of D̲a̲v̲i̲d̲
① ② ⑦ ④   ③ ⑤ ⑥ ② ③

page 26

NATIVITY SCRAMBLE

Unscramble each word and draw a line to its matching picture.

BAYB
BABY

MYAR
MARY

MNAEGR
MANGER

SATR
STAR

AGNEL
ANGEL

LMAB
LAMB

page 27

NATIVITY CROSSWORD

Use the picture clues on the next page to complete the crossword puzzle.

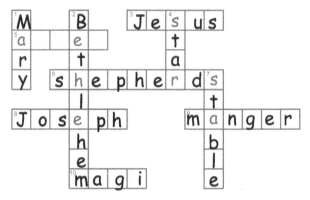

Across

3. Son of God
5. Heavenly messenger from God
6. They take care of sheep
8. Mary's husband
9. Where the infant Jesus slept
10. Wise men

Down

1. Mother of Jesus
2. The town where Jesus was born
4. This appeared in the sky over Bethlehem and guided the Magi to Jesus
7. Building that houses animals; where Jesus was born

page 28

44

DONKEY

Find and circle the two donkeys that are exactly same.

page 30

CHRISTMAS

How many words can you make using the letters in **Christmas**?

cat

art	his
mat	hat
sat	march
arm	him
	car
	star
	smart
	chair ...

page 31

CHRISTMAS
word search

Find and circle all 16 words below in the puzzle. The words go across, backward and down.

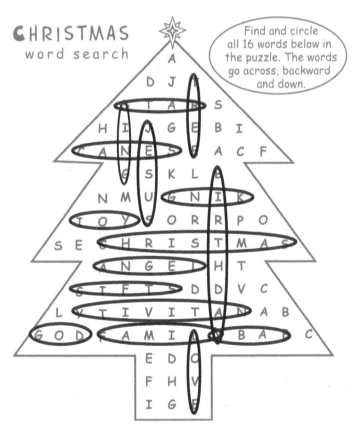

page 32

NATIVITY MAP

Fill in the puzzle with the 4 bold names of places from the nativity story.

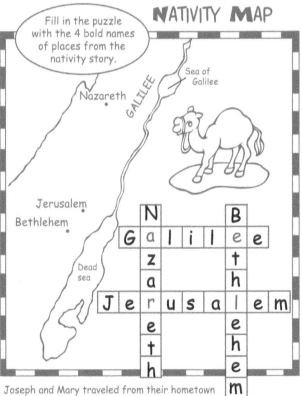

Joseph and Mary traveled from their hometown **Nazareth**, a little village in **Galilee** to **Bethlehem**, where Mary had her baby. Later, the Magi journeyed to Bethlehem by way of **Jerusalem**.

page 37